Given to:

With Love:

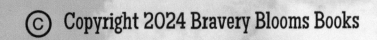
© Copyright 2024 Bravery Blooms Books

BRAVERY BLOOMS BOOKS

MY VERY FIRST AIRPLANE RIDE!

A BRAVE KID'S GUIDE TO THEIR FIRST AIRPLANE RIDE

Today is a very special day!
We are going to go on an airplane!

We will pack up our bags with the things that we need... and you can bring some of your very favorite things! We will take two bags, one to keep with you on the plane and one that will ride in the luggage compartment that we will get when we arrive!

In your carry on you might want to bring a favorite toy, or a yummy snack that you will enjoy!

When we arrive at the airport, it can be busy and loud...
It is important that you stay with a grown-up and don't wander off...

We will walk inside where we can drop off our checked bags. Your checked bags will have things that you won't need on the plane, like our jammies or clothes or toothbrushes.

The airline workers will mark our checked bags with a special tag that will have your name and destination.
Destination is a fancy word that means- where we are going. this will help the workers to know that your bag belongs with us on our plane!

The bags will go on a quick ride on a conveyor belt behind the counter to be loaded by the airport workers onto the plane.

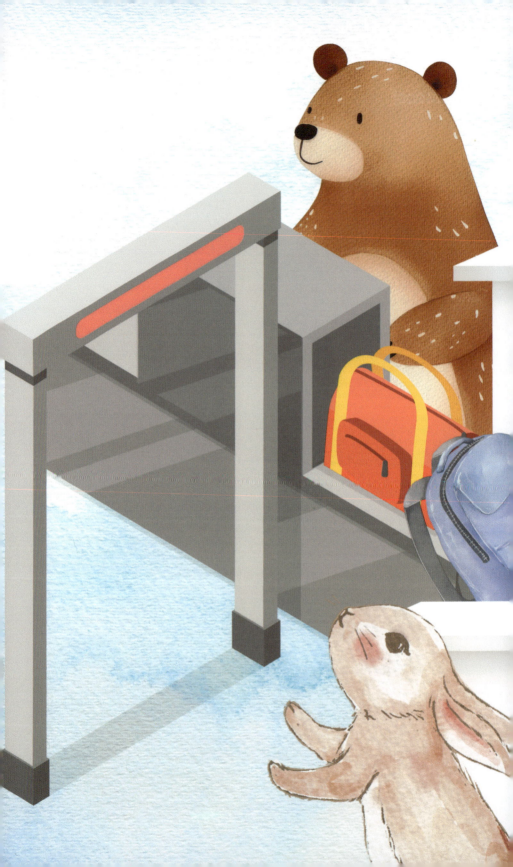

Next we will walk through a
Security Checkpoint!
The officers will scan your ticket for the plane, and ask you your name and age. I know you can be brave and tell them your name!

It's important that we listen to the officers and follow directions. They will have you walk through a metal detector and put your carry-on bag through a special x-ray machine to make sure everything on you and inside of your bag is safe for the flight.

Then we will take a walk to our gate. The gate is where we wait for our plane and hop on when it is time! There are even bathrooms next to the gate... It's a good idea to try before we get ready to FLY!

At the gate, you can often look down and see the airport workers taking the baggage on big carts to be loaded on the plane!

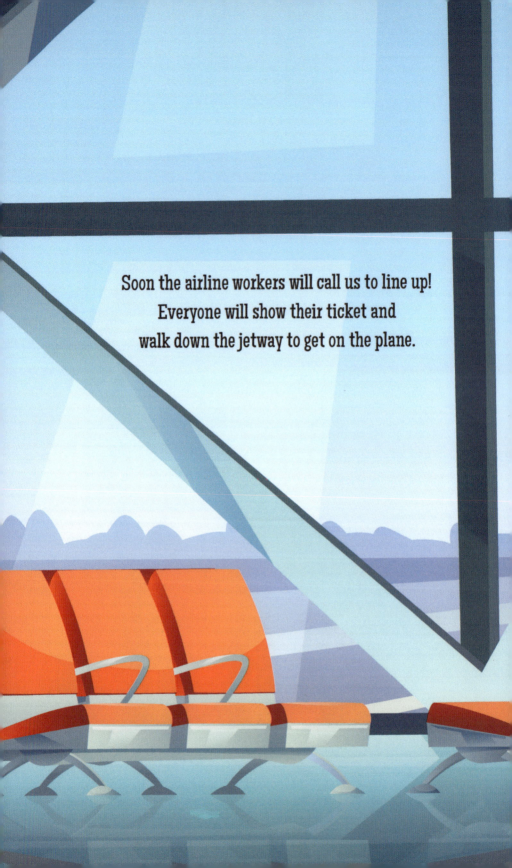
Soon the airline workers will call us to line up! Everyone will show their ticket and walk down the jetway to get on the plane.

The jetway is a long tunnel that connects to the plane. It can be warm in the summer and cold in the winter.

When you get to the end of the jetway, you will see the outside of the plane. There will be a small gap between the jetway and the door... it's fun to take a big step over the gap!

Once you get inside... you might see the Pilot in the cockpit!

The Flight attendant will help you find your seat. There are lots of people on the plane, So it is important that we don't make too much noise so everyone can hear all of the directions.

Sit back and relax...
Up Up into the sky we go!
Sometimes ears can act a little funny... and if they do... grab a snack and start to chew. The snacks will help them right away to feel better on your special flying day!

When the plane is up in the air I know you will be brave, and tell your grown-up if you feel afraid.
Your grown-up can help you take deep breaths,
snuggle with your favorite lovey, have some snacks or watch a special show. There is even a potty on the plane if you need to go!

Flying is FUN and it gets you where you are going fast!

As the airplane starts to land you will hear the wheels go zing zing as they lower down... Then a baaaadump baaaaaadump as they lower to the ground. it can be a little bumpy but You are brave... You'll have the best flight I know it's true you are the bravest YOU!

You'll do it!

You'll make it to a brand new town! You'll pick up your luggage from a baggage merry-go-round! Then off you'll go, you are adventure bound! Listening to instructions, staying close to your grown-ups, and being brave at the airport and on the plane is the very first step... and I know you will do it and have the most fun!
Because flying is fun for everyone!

Printed in Great Britain
by Amazon

48974271R00021